Primary Sources of Westward Expansion

Native American Resistance

Zachary Deibel

Cavendish
Square
New York

Library of Congress Cataloging-in-Publication Data
Names: Deibel, Zachary.
Title: Native American resistance / Zachary Deibel.
Description: New York : Cavendish Square Publishing, 2018. | Series: Primary sources of westward
expansion | Includes index.
Identifiers: ISBN 9781502626448 (library bound) | ISBN 9781502626349 (ebook)
Subjects: LCSH: Indians of North America--Wars--Juvenile literature. | Indians of North America-
-Government relations--Juvenile literature. | Indians of North America--Social conditions--Juvenile
literature.
Classification: LCC E81.K55 2018 | DDC 970.004'97--dc23

Editorial Director: David McNamara
Editor: Fletcher Doyle
Copy Editor: Nathan Heidelberger
Associate Art Director: Amy Greenan
Designer: Raúl Rodriguez
Production Coordinator: Karol Szymczuk
Photo Research: J8 Media

CONTENTS

Friends to Foes

I n 1776, leaders of the American Revolution in Philadelphia invited the Iroquois Confederacy to a session of the newly formed Continental Congress. Fearing the Natives would choose to fight for the British Empire in the Americans' war for independence, the delegates begged the Iroquois for their support. "Brothers," they pleaded in an address delivered on June 11, "we hope the friendship that is between us and you will be firm." The king of Great Britain had become upset with the Americans because "we will not let him take away from us our land, and all that we have, and give it to them, and because we will not do every thing that he bids us." They continued, "We hope you will not suffer any of your young men to join with our enemies ... that nothing may happen to make any quarrel between us." The Americans had lived on the continent for fewer than two centuries. Now, they were asking the Natives, whose **territory** and freedom they had taken for decades, for help preserving their liberty and land.

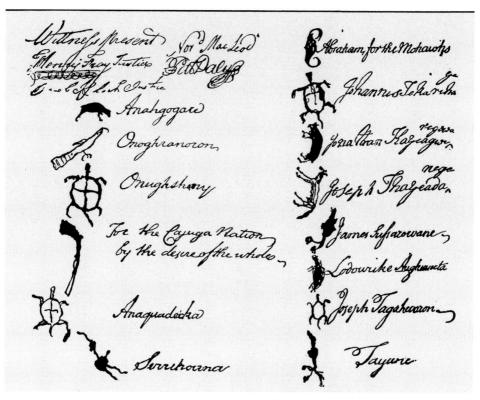

Six Nations tribal chiefs signed a document selling land to Pennsylvania with pictograms. The written signatures were added by another hand.

Throughout its existence, the United States has oppressed Native Americans in various ways. Americans occupied Native territory, forced indigenous people to relocate, used military force to push Native people from their homelands, and even waged war against several Native nations. The United States wanted to achieve a firm hold over the entire North American continent, and they saw this pursuit of coast-to-coast domination as a national destiny. Many Native Americans chose to resist this injustice. Both Native Americans and American citizens fought back against these injustices, through legal actions, protest, and armed conflict.

From 1803 to 1869, the United States saw the West as a new frontier for American society. It would provide farmland, serve an ever-growing population, bring new states into the

Union, and allow people to travel all over the country on a railroad that would span the continent. Initially, the United States negotiated with Native American nations through treaties and agreements to share much of the land. However, as politicians became more fixated on expanding the nation's territory, they betrayed previous treaties to pursue American interests.

The Native people, however, were not willing to let the United States government exploit them without resisting such injustice. These struggles eventually led to decades of brutal conflict between the United States and Native Americans. The United States would be responsible for millions of Native American deaths over the course of its history, but many courageous Native people spoke out and resisted this oppression.

Theodore Frelinghuysen led opposition to Indian removal in the US Senate.

Opposition also came from other sources. In 1830, Senator Theodore Frelinghuysen of New Jersey opposed the **Indian Removal** Act, which allowed the government to forcibly remove **Cherokees** from their homelands in the South. "Do the obligations of justice change with the color of the skin?" asked Frelinghuysen. Many Native Americans would rise up throughout history to answer Frelinghuysen's question with a resounding "No." If the United States would not treat them fairly and justly, they would fight back. And fight back they did.

CHAPTER ONE

Shared Home

The first leaders of the young United States quickly realized that the nation's relationship with Native Americans would be an important area of concern. Starting with the Treaty of Paris in 1783, which ended the Revolutionary War, the United States began to assert itself as the central power on the continent. The Natives of North America had a long history of both conflicts and alliances with many of the European powers that had established colonies. From French trade agreements to near enslavement by the Spanish, Native Americans across the continent had experienced several different approaches from European colonists. During the Revolution, some Native nations had aligned with the colonists, but many tribes fought with the British, believing the British Empire offered better chances for peace than the colonists' independent government. However, after the conflict, Native groups were forced to negotiate with the new American government.

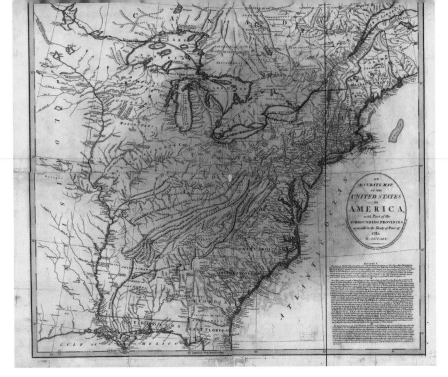

This map, drawn for the treaty with Britain that ended the American Revolution in 1783, shows the United States and its adjacent territories.

Early presidents and national political leaders aimed to achieve **assimilation** of Natives. Through this **policy**, leaders hoped to incorporate Native Americans into the population of the young nation. The first president of the United States, George Washington, and his secretary of war, Henry Knox, were the first to formulate the nation's policy toward Natives. Washington feared the expansion of Americans into Native territories would spark violence, and he knew agreements needed to be made to prevent citizens from taking Native land. In 1796, Washington passed a law aiming "to Preserve Peace on the Frontiers" that recognized Native territory as sovereign and independent, while authorizing Congress to punish any American citizen who violated the terms of any agreement that was reached. Though Washington and Knox spent most of his early presidency establishing clear boundaries between Natives and settlers, Washington's vision

Native American Resistance

for the Natives was one of inclusion. However, this proved incredibly insensitive to the liberties of the Native peoples.

In 1796, Washington published an open letter to the Cherokee Nation, explaining that he had "anxiously wished that the various Indian tribes, as well as their neighbors the white people, might enjoy in abundance all the good things." In order to do this, Washington continued, he hoped that the Cherokees would "learn those things which will make books useful to you." He wanted the Natives "to till the ground, to build good houses, and to fill them with good things, as the white people do." Washington then instructed the Natives how to farm as Americans did, establish governments similar to the United States' new republic, and discuss community issues like a democracy. "The advice I have given you is important as it regards your nation," Washington wrote. Should the Natives adopt American ways of life, "the Beloved Men of the United States will be encouraged to give the same assistance to all the Indian tribes." If they did not, Americans would not "make any further attempts to better the condition of any Indian tribes," and they would use the "richness of the soil and mildness of the air" that belonged to the Natives to further their own society. By the end of his presidency, this was what President Washington and the American government wanted. The Natives would adopt American lifestyles, or the United States would use their land and resources to improve their own country.

Seneca chief Red Jacket, wearing a peace medal, circa 1829

Program of Assimilation

Presidents after Washington pursued similar policies. In 1803, Thomas Jefferson purchased the Louisiana Territory from Napoléon Bonaparte and the French Empire. The land acquired stretched from the Ohio Valley through the southern and central United States. Though the Natives who occupied this territory did not know that the French, let alone the United States, ever claimed this land, Jefferson sent two young explorers, Meriwether Lewis and William Clark, to explore the new frontier. He instructed them to assert sovereignty, but to do so peacefully, with honorable displays to the tribes they encountered. Jefferson wanted to use this territory to provide "agriculture … manufactures … and civilization" for both Natives and frontiersmen. The West would be the arena, in Jefferson's opinion, where Americans would adopt Native populations into the growing national identity. Unfortunately, this assimilation was not a choice for Native tribes.

Lewis and Clark consult with their Shoshone guide, Sacagawea, without whom they would never have made it to the Pacific Ocean.

Jefferson's "civilization program," according to the museum at Thomas Jefferson's Monticello, aimed to both secure American lands and gradually merge Native peoples with American culture. Some of his tactics toward Native Americans, much like those of many American politicians throughout history, were manipulative. He instructed William Henry Harrison (a future president of the United States) to convince Native nations to buy land using American credit, putting them in debt to the nation for decades. Jefferson lobbied Congress to enforce laws that would promote his program as well. "In leading them thus to agriculture … and civilization; in bringing together their and our sentiments, and in preparing them ultimately to participate in the benefits of our Government," Jefferson wrote, "I trust and believe we are acting for their greatest good." Jefferson continued the paternalistic, or fatherly, image of the United States saving Natives from a savage existence. This "civilization" was not always a choice for Native Americans. However, it proved to be a more pleasant way for the United States to describe its real objective: territorial expansion.

Jefferson's successor, a fellow Virginian and the primary author of the nation's Constitution, James Madison, continued many aspects of Jefferson's "civilization program." The tribes that had agreed to American attempts at assimilation took the title the "**Five Civilized Tribes**." These groups—the Cherokees, the Chickasaws, the Choctaws, the Creeks, and the Seminoles—enjoyed a period of relative peace with the United States. However, even these groups, which had agreed to the United States' terms in nearly every agreement, would eventually fall victim to broken promises. Meanwhile, some of the Natives did not adopt the "civilization program" as readily. The **Shawnee** Nation was incredibly divided. While some factions within the Shawnees accepted assimilation, others rejected it.

One Shawnee leader who was opposed to American assimilation, Tecumseh, led an alliance of Natives against the United States. Tecumseh had a long history of opposition to American expansion. He fought against the Americans in the 1794 Battle of Fallen Timbers. He helped the Shawnees create a confederacy of Native tribes to resist the United States at the Battle of Tippecanoe in 1811. William Henry Harrison led American forces, which were ambushed by the confederacy before Tecumseh's arrival. The United States crushed the Shawnees and their allies, but Tecumseh used the Americans' brutal retaliation of burning the Native village to the ground to rally support against them.

In 1812, Tecumseh used these alliances to fight the United States alongside the British. That year, the United States went to war with Great Britain in a second struggle to assure its independence. The conflict began over British imprisonment of American soldiers, attempts to take American territory, and the British practice of encouraging Native tribes to resist and attack American settlements. Tecumseh aligned himself with Britain, expecting the empire to treat Natives better than the United States had in its early years. Tecumseh feared a North American continent completely controlled by the United States. Though the British Empire had outlawed the slave trade in 1807, the United States' economy relied on a massive force of slave labor on southern and western farms. Tecumseh feared that the same **slavery** would be extended to Natives, another oppressed minority group fighting for freedom against an expanding white nation. "How long will it be before they will tie us to a post and whip us, and make us work for them in their cornfields as they do them [African slaves]?" Tecumseh asked his allies. "Shall we wait for that moment or shall we die

Tecumseh fought against the United States.

fighting?" Tecumseh, the Shawnees, and many other Native groups did just that. Tecumseh died during the Battle of the Thames on October 5, 1813.

Refusing Demands

Though the United States would emerge from the War of 1812 victorious, resistance from Native American groups to American expansion was established. As American desire for land in the West grew, so too did the government's willingness to take tribal territory and push the Native populations out. Many Natives resisted. In 1826, the Chickasaws refused to accept American demands for land. The United States wanted the Chickasaws to move west, past the Mississippi River, and allow Americans to occupy their territory. In a speech to American officials, the Chickasaws stated, "Thinking it would not be to the advantage of the nation to cross the Mississippi, we are resolved to remain in our native country." Interestingly, the Chickasaws' resistance to American influence owed itself to the same democratic ideals for which the young nation stood. "We have to act agreeably to the voice of the [Chickasaw] people," wrote the Natives' representatives. "We cannot act contrary to the will of the [Chickasaw] nation. They are determined on staying in their native country." In this appeal, the Natives attempted to convince the American officials of their country's own hypocrisy—how could the United States be a nation based on majority rule if it did not respect others' use of the same idea? This diplomatic resistance, though rare, showed Native willingness to stand up to the United States as it tried to acquire territory.

However, the ever-changing politics within the United States would bring an end to the era of assimilation and Jefferson's "civilization program." In 1828, the Americans elected Andrew Jackson president. He promised to protect small farmers and working-class people from many different groups, including the Natives of the western frontier.

As many voters moved west, they saw a vote for Jackson as a vote for security. After all, he had fought Natives in Louisiana, Florida, and Georgia. As settlers moved west, Jackson promised to protect them from the dangers posed by Native Americans. Jackson was a firm believer in what became known as "**manifest destiny**," or the idea that the United States had a God-given right to extend its territory across the continent. This combination—Jackson's belief in American expansion, and his willingness to combat disagreeable tribes— would spell disaster for thousands of Native Americans.

Throughout the 1820s, many states and territories tried to push Natives out of areas occupied by white Americans. Georgia was particularly forceful in trying to push the Cherokees out of its state borders by force. However, in 1827, the Cherokees adopted their own "Constitution for the Government of the Cherokee Nation" in order to, as the document said, "secure to ourselves and our posterity the blessings of liberty." The constitution declared that "the lands therein are, and shall remain, the common property of the [Cherokee] Nation ... the exclusive and indefeasible property of the citizens respectively who made, or may rightfully be in possession of them." Many political leaders in Georgia and other states with sizeable Native populations were infuriated by this attempt to assert independence. In response, the United States Congress, led by its Georgian representatives, passed the Indian Removal Act of 1830. The law authorized Jackson to designate western territory for Native American occupation. "It shall and may be lawful for the President of the United States," the law said, "to cause ... any territory belonging to the United States, west of the river Mississippi ... to be divided into a suitable number of districts, for the reception of such tribes or nations of Indians as may choose to exchange the lands where they now reside."

No president had ever had this much power to designate lands for Native occupation. Even worse for the Native

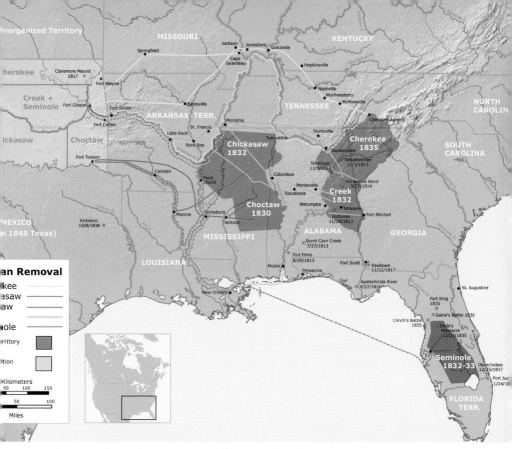

This map shows the process and the routes by which many Native Americans were forcibly removed from their territory.

Americans, the law stated that the president had full power "to exchange any or all of such districts" west of the Mississippi River "with any tribe or nation of Indians now residing within the limits of any of the states or territories … owned by the United States." In essence, the law allowed the president to force Native Americans to relocate from their land inside American states to areas picked out for them in the American West. Additionally, the law set aside $500,000 to cover the expenses of removal, which included, in Congress's estimates, the use of military force. Because the president was the commander in chief of the military, the federal government prepared to force Natives from their homes to the West.

Spanish Authority in the Southwest

In the American Southwest, around modern-day New Mexico, Native groups struggled against Spanish colonization for decades. After conquering much of Central and South America, the Spanish divided the land of the Pueblo Natives into communities governed by Spanish nobles. The Natives themselves were also allotted to the nobles as laborers. The granting of land and of the service required of the Native people living on that land was called encomienda. The allotment of Natives was called repartimiento. Native Americans worked almost as slaves in mines and on farms under the Spanish, and they were forced to convert to Christianity, live within the encomienda, and declare their loyalty to Spain. The Spanish attempted to reform this system with what was called the New Laws in 1542. This system changed the definition of repartimiento as it outlawed forced labor and required that Natives be paid for their work. The Native groups still had to provide labor, but now their days of service would be limited. However, they still were forced to abide by Spanish cultural expectations.

As the Spanish expanded into other parts of the Southwest, as well as modern-day Texas and Florida, many Natives grew restless under their rule. From 1600 to 1680, the Pueblo population declined by more than 73 percent as a result of harsh living conditions, epidemics brought about by Europeans, and conflict with their colonial rulers. In 1680, a group of Pueblos led by a charismatic leader named Popé led a rebellion against the Spanish. Hundreds of Spanish colonists and missionaries were killed in the uprising, and the Pueblos essentially pushed the Spanish from their territory. Historian Eric Foner points out, "The

A 1590 depiction of Native laborers being abused by Spanish colonists.

Pueblo **Revolt** was the most complete victory for Native Americans over Europeans and the only wholesale expulsion of settlers in the history of North America … The victorious Pueblos turned with a vengeance on all symbols of European culture, uprooting fruit trees, destroying cattle, burning churches … and wading into rivers to wash away their Catholic baptisms."

The Pueblo Revolt was not just a violent uprising—it was a resistance to and rejection of European oppression. By 1692, Pueblo leadership broke apart, and the Spanish again gained control of the territory. However, Spain had learned its lesson. In the decades following the revolt, the Spanish were far more tolerant of Native traditions and independence when they negotiated trade agreements and political alliances.

Through use of the Indian Removal Act, Jackson authorized the forced relocation of thousands of Cherokees out of Georgia. They would be marched, by the United States military, to the Oklahoma Territory. Sixteen thousand Cherokees were forced to move between 1836 and 1839. Along the way, roughly four thousand Natives died on what became known as the "Trail of Tears." American soldier John Burnett recorded the implementation of what he called "the most brutal order in the history of American warfare." Burnett described, "I saw the helpless Cherokees arrested and dragged from their homes, and driven at the bayonet point into the stockades … I saw them loaded like cattle or sheep into six hundred and forty-five wagons and started toward the west." Though the removal of these people from their homes was painful, the journey would prove even more horrific. According to Burnett, "Many of these helpless people did not have blankets and many of them had been driven from home barefooted." Burnett also remarked:

> The trail of the exiles was a trail of death …
> Men working in the fields were arrested and
> driven to the stockades. Women were dragged
> from their homes by soldiers whose language
> they could not understand. Children were often
> separated from their parents and driven into
> the stockades … A little sad-faced child had
> died and was lying on a bearskin couch and
> some women were preparing the little body for
> burial. All were arrested and driven out leaving
> the child in the cabin … In another home was
> a frail mother, apparently a widow and three
> small children, one just a baby. When told that
> she must go, the mother gathered the children
> at her feet, prayed a humble prayer in her native
> tongue, patted the old family dog on the head,

Cherokee families trek through the snow along the bitter Trail of Tears.

told the faithful creature good-by, with a baby strapped on her back and leading a child with each hand started on her exile. But the task was too great for that frail mother … She sunk and died with her baby on her back, and her other two children clinging to her hands.

The Cherokees experienced great hardship. Each of the four thousand deaths is similarly tragic—women, children, and men of all ages died from disease and fatigue. The march, overseen by United States soldiers, marked a key point in Native American removal. Though the United States began its relations with Native Americans focused on assimilation, the nation soon turned to a policy of removing Natives from territory that it wanted to hold or acquire. Historian Howard Zinn explains, however, that removal was not an immediate policy. "The Indians would not be 'forced' to go west. But if they chose to stay, they would have to abide by state laws, which destroyed their tribal and personal rights and made them subject to endless harassment and invasion by white settlers coveting their land." However, when they refused, the federal government forced these nations from their homelands. The United States wanted to expand, at whatever cost.

Fighting Forced Removal

Many Native groups resisted removal, however, and several conflicts erupted in response to the Indian Removal Act and the Trail of Tears. The Seminole Nation waged a seven-year war against the United States from 1835 to 1842, resisting attempts to relocate their tribes west of the Mississippi. The war cost the United States $20 million, and despite the Seminoles' eventual defeat, it revealed Native American willingness to oppose American injustices.

Speckled Snake, a Creek chief, opposed Jackson's attempts to negotiate their removal westward. In his opposition speech, Speckled Snake explained:

> Our great father [Jackson] says that our bad men have made his heart bleed, for the murder of one of his white children. Yet where are the red children which he loves, once as numerous as the leaves of the forest? How many have been murdered by his warriors? How many have been crushed beneath his own footsteps?

Speckled Snake, and other Natives, actively opposed negotiations with the United States, hoping to prevent the same forced migrations that would be practiced upon the Cherokees.

Even Native groups as far away as the Northeast opposed removal. William Apess, a Pequot Native and ordained Methodist minister, wrote a Christian analysis of Native affairs called "An Indian's Looking Glass for the White Man." In it, Apess used his advanced knowledge of Christian philosophy to point out the ways in which American policies toward Natives were morally wrong. "Why are we [Natives] not protected in our persons and property throughout the Union?" Apess asked. God, Apess summarized, protected all his children—did this not include the Cherokees, or any other group of Native Americans? Surely Christians could not practice terrible actions like those of the people who carried out the Trail of Tears.

In the words of historian Eric Foner, "Removal was the alternative to coexistence." Though the United States initially wanted to bring Native Americans into American society, the country continued to expand and pursue its own interests above all else. Equal treatment of many people—women, African Americans, and Native Americans—was never one of its objectives. Instead, the nation wanted to acquire territory, assert its dominance, defend itself, and acquire resources. The policy of Native American removal became necessary, in the minds of America's politicians, to achieve these objectives. The Natives had to be relocated, even if some of their rights were taken away, their property confiscated, and, in some cases, their lives sacrificed for American progress. However, as John Burnett pointed out, "Murder is murder whether committed by the villain skulking in the dark or by uniformed men stepping to the strains of martial music." By 1840, the United States had fully transitioned from a policy of assimilation to one of removal and relocation, which often resulted in murder and devastation. However, Native Americans would continue to resist these injustices through political and military action well into the twentieth century.

CHAPTER TWO

Fighting to Keep Land

T hroughout the 1840s, the United States clashed with Native groups across the western frontier. As Americans began moving westward, the Natives became increasingly concerned that their territory, resources, and societies would no longer be safe. In 1846, the **Sioux** petitioned President James K. Polk for payment because American settlers had destroyed and confiscated much of their land. "The Emigrants going over the mountains from the United States," the Sioux explained, "have been the cause that Buffalo have in great measure left our hunting grounds, thereby causing us to go into the country of our enemies to hunt, exposing our lives daily for the necessary subsistence of our wives and children and getting killed on several occasions." Polk ignored the Sioux, and the tribe began to force white settlers to pay as they poured into Sioux lands. Fearing an extended conflict, the United States refused to send federal troops to protect the settlers. Open warfare with the Sioux, however, would break out after the **Civil War**.

Railroad workers and miners move westward in search of new opportunities.

In 1848, American miners discovered gold in California. This drew thousands of Americans westward as they left crowded cities in the East for the promise of opportunity on the frontier. However, this also led to more direct conflict between American settlers and Natives west of the Mississippi. As these settlers moved west, they created settlements that often violated previous agreements between the Native Americans and the United States government.

However, confiscation of territory was not the only effect of American expansion west. In 1847, authorities in California created a "certificate and pass system" that placed Native groups within the territory in a peonage system. This system regulated their travel and labor rights. Eventually, the peonage system became a form of Native slavery; Californians sold thousands of Natives into slavery to settlers and other Native tribes. Similarly, many Mormon settlers became heavily involved in a slave trade with the Utes in modern-day Utah. Settlers also carried diseases with them that devastated Native American populations. Americans took not only territory from the tribes—they aimed to take their society away as well. In California, as a result of American movement westward, the Native population went from 150,000 in 1849 to only 30,000 in 1860.

Native groups continued to resist expansion. In 1847, two Californian ranchers named Andrew Kelsey and Charles Stone purchased territory from a Mexican farmer and looked for gold through the use of a group of Pomo Natives as slave labor. Kelsey and Stone treated their laborers with extreme cruelty. In 1ate 1849, a Pomo chief led a small group in an attack that killed Kelsey and Stone. However, the United States sought revenge. In 1850, Army Lieutenant Nathaniel Lyon attacked a small island village of Pomo natives on Clear Lake in California with cannons and heavy artillery. The village was a small settlement of families that had nothing to do with the killings of Stone and Kelsey. Men, women, and children were killed as they attempted to escape. According to one Pomo account, "One lady told me she saw two white men coming, their guns up in the air and on their guns hung a little girl. They brought it to the creek and threw it in the water … When they gathered the dead they found all the little ones were killed by being stabbed." Meanwhile, in the 1850 Mariposa War, six different tribes waged open warfare against Californian authorities to prevent their land from being swallowed up in the gold rush.

Even though the Clear Lake Pomos had no connection to the killings of Kelsey and Stone, the American military still carried out this horrific attack to put an end to Native resistance. Actions like the Clear Lake Massacre became normal for American settlers during the gold rush. In 1851, the governor of California, Peter Burnett, told the people of the new state in his State of the State address:

> The two races cannot live in the same vicinity in peace … War and theft are established customs among the Indian races generally, as they are among all poor and savage tribes …

> That a war of extermination will continue to be
> waged between the races until the Indian race
> becomes extinct must be expected … Situated as
> California is, we must expect a long continued
> and harassing irregular warfare with the Indians
> upon our borders.

Ironically, Burnett argues that Native Americans are inclined to steal and wage war—practices that had allowed the United States to acquire California in the first place. The speech shows, however, that the Americans would counter Native resistance with brutal force.

No Mercy Ordered

Both the **Cheyenne** and **Navajo** tribes resisted the United States as its military prepared to engage in the Civil War. As Union soldiers occupied territory, they faced resistance from the Navajo led by a chief named Manuelito. The Navajos raided American forts in an attempt to take back supplies stolen by United States soldiers, but they were often defeated. In 1860, they led a massive assault on Fort Defiance in New Mexico. They came close to defeating the American troops, and despite their eventual retreat, they believed they had, in the words of historian Dee Brown, "taught the soldiers a good lesson." In 1861, the Navajos came to an agreement with the United States at Fort Fauntleroy to establish peace.

In 1862, however, General James Carleton and his lieutenant, Kit Carson, began attacking Apache and Navajo Natives in the region. In an attempt to secure what Carleton called the "princely realm" of land, "a magnificent pastoral and mineral country" for the United States after the war, he issued an order to his soldiers: "There is to be no council held with the Indians, nor any talks. The men are to be slain whenever and wherever they can be found. The women and children may be taken as prisoners." These captives would then be

Manuelito led Navajo resistance efforts.

imprisoned on a **reservation** in the Pecos Mountains. After he carried out this assault on the Apaches, the Navajos considered how to respond to Carleton's aggression. He demanded the Navajos give up their land, and he issued stern warnings to the tribe. "After that day [July 20, 1862]," Carleton ordered, "every Navajo that is seen will be considered as hostile and treated accordingly." However, no Navajos surrendered. In an act of defiance, they aimed to resist the Americans' unjust stealing of their territory. Carleton and Carson led assaults on the Navajo through 1862 and 1863, burning Navajo homes, destroying Navajo fields, and starving the Navajo villagers. Eventually, the Navajos were forced to surrender to Carleton and Carson's forces, fearing the extermination of their people.

In 1862, the United States Congress established Fort Sumner at Bosque Redondo, New Mexico, to serve as the first official Native American reservation west of the Oklahoma Territory. They wanted to march the Apache and Navajo people to the reservation, where they would farm the area, go to American schools, and be forced to adopt Christianity. Not all Navajos agreed to these terms, however. In 1864, they joined with the remaining Apaches to stand against Carson's army at the Battle of Canyon de Chelly. After they were defeated by the United States Army, Carson ordered their property destroyed and sent them on a forced march west to the Bosque Redondo reservation. About 8,500 Natives were marched 300 miles (480 kilometers), during which

200 Navajos died. Many more died upon arriving at the reservation, which, according to one historian, "turned into a virtual prison camp for the Indians."

The "Long Walk" of the Navajos was only the beginning of the Natives' trials. The reservation proved just as horrific. A. B. Norton, a supervisor of the reservation, recorded some of the dire conditions in his accounts. "The water is black … and scarcely bearable to the taste, and said by the Indians to be unhealthy, because one-fourth of their population have been swept off by disease." Even Norton understood the reservation was a failure.

> The sooner it [the reservation] is abandoned and the Indians removed, the better … Would any sensible man select a spot for a reservation for eight thousand Indians where the water is scarcely bearable, where the soil is poor and cold … O! Let them go back, or take them to where they can have good cool water to drink, wood plenty to keep them from freezing to death, and where the soil will produce something for them to eat.

Many Natives resisted capture. Nearly all Apaches escaped military oversight, and the reservation soon became too much to manage for the American forces.

After Norton's account reached the nation's leaders, the United States decided to close the reservation and let the Navajos return home. Manuelito recalled their journey back:

> The nights and days were long before it came time for us to go to our homes … The day before we were to start we went a little way towards home, because we were so anxious to start. We came back and the Americans gave us a little stock [food] and we thanked them for that … We were in such a hurry. When we saw the top of the mountain from Albuquerque we wondered if it was our mountain, and we felt like talking to the ground, we loved it so, and some of the old men and women cried with joy when they reached their homes.

On Trial for Murder

In the 1862 Great Sioux Uprising, the Dakota Sioux led a massively coordinated resistance effort against Union soldiers in the Great Plains. However, the effort proved tragic for the Dakotas. After the Dakotas surrendered to the army, the United States began a military tribunal to try the Natives for murder. In the end, President Abraham Lincoln ordered the execution of thirty-eight Dakotas for their acts. "Anxious to not act with so much clemency as to encourage another outbreak," Lincoln explained in an address to the United States Senate, "nor with so much severity as to be real cruelty … I ordered … the execution of such [Natives] as had been proved guilty" of massacre. This remains the largest single execution in United States history. Before his execution, the Dakota warrior Hdainyanka wrote to their Chief Wabasha:

> You have deceived me. You told me that if we followed the advice of General Sibley, and gave

A Woman Warrior

Buffalo Calf Road Woman

I n 1876, during the Sioux Wars that resulted from American expansion west, the Sioux fought fiercely against the United States. At the Battles of Rosebud and Little Bighorn, the Natives defeated the American forces. A young Cheyenne named Buffalo Calf Road Woman rode with her tribesmen into battle. She was a brave warrior, who fought valiantly for the Sioux and Cheyenne forces. According to a woman in the Cheyenne tribe, Buffalo Calf Road Woman "was also with the warriors when they went from the Reno creek camp to fight the soldiers far up Rosebud creek about a week before." After winning key victories, she also led her people in retreat, helping protect them from the American forces on their trail. Buffalo Calf Road Woman's people were captured in 1877. They surrendered, and the United States forced them to march 1,500 miles (2,414 km) to Oklahoma. Buffalo Calf Road Woman assisted in helping the Cheyenne escape. However, they were eventually hunted down and imprisoned in Montana. They were imprisoned at Fort Keogh, and Buffalo Calf Road Woman died in 1879. Her husband, Black Coyote, killed himself out of sadness after her death. Though she suffered a tragic death, her heroism served as an example to her Native people for decades.

ourselves up to the whites, all would be well; no innocent man would be injured. I have not killed, wounded or injured a white man, or any white persons. I have not participated in the plunder of their property; and yet today I am set apart for execution, and must die in a few days, while men who are guilty will remain in prison. My wife is your daughter, my children are your grandchildren. I leave them all in your care and under your protection. Do not let them suffer; and when my children are grown up, let them know that their father died because he followed the advice of his chief, and without having the blood of a white man to answer for to the Great Spirit.

After the executions, it became clear that some of those who were killed had been mistakenly hanged. However, as Lincoln indicated, the United States was more concerned with setting an example to other Native tribes than making sure justice was upheld.

The Sand Creek Massacre

During the Civil War, the United States began building the transcontinental railroad, a massive project that would link both coasts of the nation by train. However, the territory it passed through was home to thousands of Native Americans. During construction, conflict between Americans and the resident Natives continued. In 1864, the US Army invited the Cheyennes to settle at Sand Creek, Colorado. These Natives proved an obstacle to the railroad's construction, as their lands were valuable territory to the railroad companies. Unsurprisingly, the Americans' invitation was a trap. The small battalion at Sand Creek had ordered reinforcements, and the cavalry that arrived under Colonel John Chivington was tasked by Colorado governor John Evans with "the sole purpose of fighting Indians." The massacre was brutal. As Robert Bent, a guide and an eyewitness, recounted:

> After the firing the warriors put the squaws [now considered an offensive term for Native American women] and children together, and surrounded them to protect them. I saw five squaws under a bank for shelter. When troops came up to them they ran out and showed their persons, to let the soldiers know they were squaws and begged for mercy, but the soldiers shot them all … There were some thirty or forty squaws collected in a hole for protection; they sent out a little girl about six years old with a white flag on a stick; she had not proceeded but a few steps when she was shot and killed. All the squaws in that hole were afterwards killed … Every one I saw dead was scalped. I saw one squaw cut open with an unborn child, as I thought, lying by her side. Captain Soule afterwards told me that such was the fact … I saw quite a number of infants in arms killed with their mothers.

Railroads and Revenge

These Natives never had a chance to fight back, but the group attacked included very few warriors. Nonetheless, other groups struck back. An alliance of Sioux, Arapaho, and Cheyenne fighters destroyed the town of Julesburg in Colorado. They destroyed telegraph stations and public buildings. They burned the city to the ground, killing civilians and soldiers alike. They wanted to halt American construction of the railroad, while also taking revenge for the military's atrocities at Sand Creek.

This 1867 sketch shows Cheyennes attacking a Union Pacific Railroad work crew.

These back-and-forth skirmishes continued throughout the railroad's construction. In 1866, the Sioux attacked American forces along the Bozeman Trail. After the Americans were trapped by an ambush of Cheyenne, Sioux, and Miniconjous Natives led by Red Cloud, a Sioux chief, none survived. General William Tecumseh Sherman reportedly remarked, "We must act with vindictive earnestness against the Sioux, even to their extermination, men, women, children." This retribution, however, would not come until the end of the nineteenth century. Resistance to the railroad continued. Cheyenne raiders derailed a train in 1867, leading to the death of many crew members. In 1868, the Sioux derailed a train, destroying telegraph lines and killing two crewmen.

However, the progress of the railroad proved too overwhelming. The United States completed the railroad in 1869, bringing in floods of new settlers for decades. The completion of the railroad, however, was not the end of Native resistance to American expansion. These tribes had been betrayed by American **diplomacy**. Treaties negotiated had been betrayed, and the Natives aimed to retake their land. However, the United States, as it often did, ignored its promises to Native Americans. It would continue to move Natives onto reservations, threaten warfare with those who resisted, and destroy those who refused.

CHAPTER THREE

Treaties
and Betrayal

I n 1784, the United States negotiated treaties with the
Cherokee, Choctaw, and Chickasaw tribes that reduced
the Native Americans' lands, while also assuring these
peoples that Americans would not take any more of their
lands. In the same year, the Treaty of Fort Stanwix guaranteed
protection and peace to "the Six Nations" of the Iroquois,
many of whom had fought with British forces during the
American Revolution. In each case, the treaties required
the Natives to give up land in order to enjoy peace with the
Americans. At Fort Stanwix, which is in Central New York,
the treaty mandated "that the Six Nations shall and do yield
to the United States, all claims to the country west of the
said boundary, and then they shall be secured in the peaceful
possession of the lands they inhabit." In a 1785 treaty with
several Native tribes, including the Wiandots, the Chippewas,
and the Ottawas, the United States required that "Indian
nations do acknowledge themselves and all their tribes to be

under the protection of the United States and of no other sovereign whatsoever." This meant they were to answer to only the American nation, and they could have political ties with neither foreign powers nor within their own tribal traditions. These treaties were not simply peaceful agreements—they were manipulative attempts at limiting the freedom of Native Americans to live according to their own traditions.

Native American resistance often occurred as a result of broken treaties with the United States. From its first negotiations, the United States proved unreliable when it came to honoring agreements with Native American tribes. From 1790 to 1795, the United States passed a series of Indian Trade and Intercourse Acts. These laws attempted to prevent American citizens from interacting with Natives. President George Washington feared that extended conflict with Native Americans would prevent the United States from being able to thrive as a new nation. The first of these acts began:

The Shawnee lost the Battle of Fallen Timbers.

> That no person shall be permitted to carry on any trade or intercourse with the Indian tribes, without a license for that purpose under the hand and seal of the superintendent of the department, or of such other person as the President of the United States shall appoint for that purpose.

This practice pleased Natives, as they had, too often, faced aggression and dishonesty from European and American settlers. However, these laws would not prevent American settlers or government officials from seeking to acquire the Natives' land.

In 1794, General "Mad" Anthony Wayne led troops into Shawnee territory in the Ohio Valley, meeting them at the Battle of Fallen Timbers. After the battle, the Treaty of Greenville, signed in 1795, forced Natives in the Ohio Territory to cede, or give up, their land to the United States. This began a long history of American officials using a combination of treaty negotiations and warfare to see that their interests were achieved. The treaties themselves, however, were frequently dishonestly acquired. "Often, a treaty was agreed to by only a small portion of the tribe," historian Eric Foner observes. "The whole tribe was then forced to accept its legitimacy.

THE GREENVILLE TREATY LINE

The Treaty of Greenville established this border between US and Native land.

This became a central element of many conflicts between the United States and Native Americans. In 1805, the United States secured territory from the Chickasaws, who were bankrupted by dishonest American traders. The treaty begins,

> Whereas the Chickasaw nation of Indians have been for some time embarrassed by heavy debts due to their merchants and traders, and

being destitute of funds to effect important improvements in their country, they have agreed and do hereby agree to cede to the United States, and forever quit claim to the tract of country included within the following bounds …

Here, the treaty makes the acquisition of Chickasaw territory seem charitable. However, the Chickasaws' financial woes had been caused by dealings with the United States. The United States offered "to make the following payments, to wit: Twenty thousand dollars for the use of the nation at large, and for the payment of the debts due to their merchants and traders." They would offer more money for the land, but the true cost of these offerings would be felt for decades by Native tribes across the continent.

Gaining Dominance

The War of 1812 secured American dominance on the continent for good. Despite early British and Native victories, after the Americans successfully defended Lake Erie in 1813, the British and Native forces lost a key conflict at the Battle of the Thames. The Shawnee chief Tecumseh was killed in the conflict. A young Tennessee general in the American army named Andrew Jackson became an instant celebrity after an impressive victory over the British and Creek Nation in the Battle of New Orleans. "The power of the Creeks is forever broken," Jackson commented after the conflict. He would spend the rest of his military and political career continuing to pursue his crusade against the country's Native Americans, using force and coercion to push them from their homelands and claim the territory for the United States.

After the United States won the Battle of Fort McHenry in 1814, the war crawled to a slow end. At the signing of the Treaty of Ghent, the British ceded control of American territory, preserving the territories each nation had controlled before the conflict. The treaty, however, contained no provision protecting Native American territories. Defeated by the American military and betrayed by the British Empire, Natives on America's frontier found themselves at the mercy of American expansion. From 1815 until 1830, the United States gradually claimed Native territory through both treaty negotiations and military expansion. In 1818, Andrew Jackson invaded Florida (Spanish territory) to take revenge on the Seminoles, who had conflicts over territory with American settlers. In the same year, the United States convinced representatives of the Chickasaw Nation to cede territory to the United States throughout the western frontiers of Tennessee and southern Ohio. In 1828, the United States coerced the Potawatomis of Michigan and the Great Lakes to give up their territory, while also noting that they "may be compelled to remove west of the Mississippi."

The War of 1812 set a precedent for American response to Native American resistance. Natives could meet Americans' demands, or face conflict. Despite any treaties or agreements, the Natives would be subjected to the immediate and short-term needs of the growing nation. Legal disagreements would not get in the way. Nonetheless, Native tribes still used legal protest as a means of voicing their resistance and opposition

In 1832, a missionary named Samuel Worcester sued the state of Georgia over its removal of the Cherokees. He eventually took his case to the United States Supreme Court. Worcester was sentenced to jail by Georgia's state courts because he had violated a law forbidding white Americans from living with Natives. This law, among Georgia's other rules regarding Natives, was meant to exclude Natives from American society and, eventually, force them to leave. However, Worcester and his attorneys argued that the Cherokee Nation had established its own constitution.

It should be considered an independent, free nation. Therefore, the United States could not force the Cherokees from their land without openly declaring war. In a historic Supreme Court ruling, Chief Justice John Marshall agreed. "He [Worcester] is not less entitled to the protection of the Constitution, laws, and treaties of his country [the Cherokee Nation]," Marshall confirmed. "The Cherokee

Cherokee leader John Ross petitioned for a halt to the Indian removal policy.

Nation, then, is a distinct community occupying its own territory … in which the laws of Georgia can have no force." The only power that could negotiate with the Cherokees was the federal government, according to Marshall. The Cherokees were a separate, free, and independent nation; the United States had to treat it as such.

Jackson Ignores Court

However, in infamous disregard for the Constitution and the separation of powers between branches of the federal government, Jackson supposedly responded to Marshall's ruling by saying, "John Marshall has made his decision; now let him enforce it." Jackson carried out the removal of Cherokees through the Trail of Tears, but many resisted. Cherokee chief John Ross petitioned Congress in an open letter criticizing the United States for its terrible actions. "We are stripped of every attribute of freedom," Ross explained. "Our property may be plundered before our eyes, violence may be committed on our persons, even our lives may be taken away, and there is none to regard our complaints." He argued that the Cherokees had lost their nation, they had lost their freedom, and they had been "deprived of membership in the human family." This had not been a voiceless struggle. Ross pointed out how "the government of the United States, in the face of our earnest, solemn, and reiterated protests," ignored the wishes and liberties of the Native people. Ross even referenced the more diplomatic approaches of George Washington and Thomas Jefferson.

> We have read their communications ... We have practiced their precepts [suggestions] with success ... The wildness of the forest has given place to comfortable dwellings ... We have learned your religion also. ... Spare our people! Spare the wreck of our prosperity!

In open protest to the United States Congress, Ross attempted to convince Americans of the injustice being committed by their own government.

The United States passed the 1834 Indian Trade and Intercourse Act, which forbade any settlers from occupying Native land in Wisconsin and Iowa. It also banned any unapproved trade with the tribes there, and it protected these groups' sovereignty. However, after American settlers expanded into the territory, the United States chose to defend its law-breaking citizens rather than adhere to its agreements. Congress adjusted the law, renegotiated the treaties, and slowly saw Americans overrun the Natives' territories.

In 1848, the United States signed the Treaty of Guadalupe Hidalgo, which ended the Mexican-American War. This also officially gave the United States access to massive amounts of territory in the West. The main issue, among Americans, with this new territory was the slavery question: would the United States allow slavery to expand into the western territories? This question would eventually tear the United States apart, and the Civil War broke out in 1861, when the Southern

Breaking the Fort Laramie Treaty

In 1868, the United States negotiated a treaty with the Sioux of North and South Dakota. Since Americans had first migrated westward, the Sioux and other tribes had fiercely defended the area around the Dakotas called the Black Hills. This region was especially sacred to these nations. After years of conflict, Congress released the "Report on the Condition of Indian Tribes," which eventually led to the government seeking peace with these groups. The treaty stated, "From this day forward all war between the parties to this agreement [the Sioux and the United States] shall forever cease."

The United States promised the Black Hills would be "set apart for the absolute and undisturbed use and occupation of the Indians herein named [the Sioux]." The treaty continued, "No persons … may be authorized to enter upon Indian reservations." However, in 1874, General George Custer led a group of American soldiers and miners into the Black Hills in order to see if the region contained any gold. When they found out that it did, American miners began moving into the region. When the intruders were attacked by Sioux defenders, the United States ordered the army to invade the region, leading to an extended war between the United States and the Sioux people.

General William T. Sherman and others meet with Native American chiefs, circa 1868, to negotiate the Fort Laramie Treaty.

states formed the Confederate States of America and seceded from the nation. The war, despite being a conflict between Americans, had a severe impact on Native Americans across the country. The Navajos were among the tribes who felt the effects of war. "In New Mexico," historian Andrés Reséndez observed, "the Civil War led to the greatest Indian slavery boom in the territory's history." Before, during, and after the conflict, Native Americans in the Southwest struggled against enslavement at the hands, often, of an army that aimed to end slavery in other parts of the nation. Many of these Navajos were forced into service in the army. Though many resisted by attacking Union soldiers, the tide of war overwhelmed the overmatched Natives.

In this instance, as was the case in many of these agreements, Native Americans were expected to adhere to a treaty that was entirely unfair. The Treaty of Guadalupe Hidalgo had transferred territory from Mexico to the United States. Neither of these nations had the authority to do so. The land had been occupied by tribes such as the Navajos, the Chumash, and the Apaches for centuries. However, the United States continued its practice of treaty negotiation only to betray the treaty years later. On the condition that no settlers would interfere with the Apaches, the United States demanded the Natives "acknowledge and declare that they are lawfully and exclusively under the laws, jurisdiction, and government of the United States of America, and [submit] to its power and authority." However, the United States would betray this agreement, and American wars with the Apaches would be waged throughout the decade.

Payments Not Made

In 1851, the United States reached agreements with the Cheyenne, Arapaho, and Crow tribes to allow Americans to establish roads and military posts in their territory. They would not be permitted to settle there. However, after the

Little Crow led Sioux resistance after American betrayals of its treaties.

gold rush, the United States began taking over territory
without apology. Many Natives, including the Dakota Sioux,
clashed with Union soldiers over these treaty betrayals.
The United States had signed a treaty with the Dakotas
in 1851, where their leader, Taoyateduta, or Little Crow,
gave up territory in exchange for peace and payment from
the Americans. However, the Americans never made the
payments. In 1862, Little Crow reluctantly led an assault on
the United States, thinking its conflict with the Confederacy
would make it vulnerable. Additionally, the Dakotas thought
it might convince the United States to fulfill promises made
in the 1851 treaty. However, Little Crow was worried about
the Dakotas' ability to win such an uprising. Before beginning
their resistance movement, Little Crow addressed his people:

Native American Resistance

Taoyateduta is not a coward, and he is not a fool! … We are only little herds of buffalo left scattered; the great herds that once covered the prairies are no more. See!—the white men are like the locusts when they fly so thick that the whole sky is a snowstorm. You may kill one—two—ten; yes, as many as the leaves in the forest yonder, and their brothers will not miss them. Kill one—two—ten, and ten times ten will come to kill you. Count your fingers all day long and white men with guns in their hands will come faster than you can count. Yes; they fight among themselves—away off. Do you hear the thunder of their big guns? … Yes; they fight among themselves, but if you strike at them they will all turn on you and devour you and your women and little children just as the locusts in their time fall on the trees and devour all the leaves in one day. You are fools … You will die like the rabbits when the hungry wolves hunt them in the Hard Moon.

Heroically, Little Crow ended his speech saying, "Taoyateduta is not a coward: he will die with you." In what came to be known as the Great Sioux Uprising, the United States Army destroyed the Dakota forces, and Little Crow was killed by American settlers in 1863, after he and the few remaining Sioux warriors returned to their devastated home. This was only the beginning of the travesty for the Sioux peoples. However, it was another example of their willingness to resist the injustices committed by the United States against their people. These injustices were truly just that—violations of the principles of justice, contract, and fairness for which the United States supposedly stood. Instead, the United States violated its agreements, and Native Americans had no choice but to resist and, often, rebel.

End of Resistance

From the end of the Civil War until the early twentieth century, the United States forcibly acquired territory from Native tribes until most had been relocated to reservations or exterminated by the military. The motivations were many: America became more populated, politicians looked for ways to acquire more resources for the nation, and the United States pursued, at all costs, its "manifest destiny" to dominate the continent from coast to coast. "Between 1860 and 1910, the United States Army, wiping out the Indian villages on the Great Plains, paved the way for the railroads [carrying trains full of Americans] to move in and take the best land," historian Howard Zinn observes. Throughout this period, Native Americans fell victim to the forced migration, political conflict, and open warfare carried out by the United States.

With the nation, aided by the end of the Civil War and the completion of a transcontinental railroad, expanding rapidly, Congress attempted to end conflicts with the Native

The Nez Percé leader Chief Joseph spoke to Congress on behalf of Native Americans.

Americans. However, peace would only be considered on terms set forth by the United States. In an act passed on July 20, 1867, a commission was appointed to meet with hostile tribes, to discover their grievances, and to sign treaties that would "remove all just causes of complaint on their part."

Money was set aside to help any Natives who left hostile tribes and relocated to a designated reservation. However, if the Native groups refused to go to a reservation:

The 1872 painting titled *American Progress* depicts Lady Liberty, the American people, and American trains moving westward while Natives flee.

… then the Secretary of War, under the direction of the President, is hereby authorized to accept the services of mounted volunteers from the Governors of the several States and Territories, in organized companies and battalions, not exceeding four thousand men in number, and for such term of service as, in his judgment, may be necessary for the suppression of Indian hostilities.

Later actions also made it clear that only one side would be held to the terms of a treaty. An example of this was the breaking of the Fort Laramie Treaty signed with the Sioux. Among the conditions for the Sioux agreeing to move to the Great Sioux Reservation was that the Black Hills be included in the reservation. The Sioux considered the Black Hills sacred, and the land was reserved for their use only. This agreement lasted only until 1874, when General George Armstrong Custer led a mining expedition that found gold in the Black Hills. Custer was ordered to move the Sioux off the land, sparking a bloody war that would include some decisive defeats of US forces.

Other acts subjected Native Americans to laws passed by Congress and took away their rights as the different, diverse nations they were. The Natives would now be treated as a collective group, not individual societies. The United States had robbed the Native Americans of their independence, and it was openly discriminating against them as a segment of the American population. Even Francis Walker, commissioner of Indian Affairs, called them "wild beasts" and "savages" in November 1872.

Change in Tactics

In 1874, the United States led an assault on the Comanche, Kiowa, Southern Cheyenne, and Arapaho tribes. The goal was to force these Natives back onto reservations. In 1875, after dozens of battles, the Comanches had no choice but to surrender, and their way of life was forever destroyed.

Other tribes fell victim to this approach after 1871. In 1863, the United States had negotiated treaties with the **Nez Percés**, taking nearly three-fourths of the tribe's remaining territory in the Pacific Northwest. In 1871, the Nez Percés' new chief, Young Joseph (later known as Chief Joseph), refused to comply with American orders to move to a new reservation in Idaho. Young Joseph stated:

> Neither lawyer nor any other chief had authority
> to sell this land … It has always belonged to
> my people. It came unclouded to them from
> our fathers, and we will defend this land as long

Victims of Genocide?

Native Americans experienced extreme oppression and injustice throughout their history of interactions with the United States. However, the destruction of Native communities began far earlier than their first negotiations with Americans. Starting in the fifteenth century, Native peoples clashed with invading Europeans who wanted to acquire riches and territory to expand their empires. In 1500, an estimated 12 million Natives occupied the continent of North America. By 1900, their population had dwindled to 237,000.

Throughout their modern history, Native North Americans have been subjected to **genocide**—a massive, organized extermination of a specific segment of the population. At the hands of the French, Spanish, English, and American authorities, Native populations were erased by military conquest, spread of infectious diseases, and forced migrations.

One historian writes that Native Americans experienced the "worst human holocaust the world had ever witnessed, roaring across two continents non-stop for four centuries and consuming ... tens of millions of people."

Big Foot, leader of the Sioux, lies frozen where he died at Wounded Knee.

In almost every case, these people experienced genocidal violence for refusing to allow other people to take over their lands and destroy their societies.

This depiction of the Battle of Little Bighorn displays the American troops and George Armstrong Custer as heroic victims of a brutal assault.

as a drop of Indian blood warms the hearts of our men.

American soldiers arrived in 1877 to force the Nez Percés onto the reservation. Joseph and his forces defeated the forces under the command of General Oliver Otis Howard. After a series of prolonged conflicts, however, the Nez Percés were forced to surrender. They lacked supplies, ammunition, and firepower to resist forever. Though the American forces had initially agreed to allow the Nez Percés to stay on the land in Idaho, they were forcibly marched 265 miles (426 km) to Kansas after General William Tecumseh Sherman ordered it so. Chief Joseph travelled to Washington, DC, in 1879 to ask for safe return to Idaho. Though the politicians enjoyed Chief Joseph's visit and marveled at his civility, the Nez Percé leader was determined to make them feel his frustration. He said:

> Good words will not give my people good health and stop them from dying. Good word will not get my people a home where they can live in peace and take care of themselves. I am tired of talk that comes to nothing. It makes my heart sick when I remember all the good words and all the broken promises … I have asked some of the great white chiefs [United States leaders] where they get their authority to say to the Indian that he shall stay in one place, while he sees white men going where they please. They cannot tell me.

Instead of allowing the small Nez Percé tribe to return to Idaho, Congress relocated them from a reservation in Kansas to one in Oklahoma. In 1885, they were permitted to return to their homeland. By that point, there were only 287 Nez Percés remaining. Joseph lived on the reservation until 1904 when, according to his doctor, he died of "a broken heart."

Revenge for Custer

The century would not end without another tragic story of Native destruction. In 1876, the Sioux waged a massive resistance against American expansion into the Black Hills. Sioux chiefs Crazy Horse and Sitting Bull led various assaults on the American military. On June 25, at the Battle of Little Bighorn in the Montana Territory, the Sioux routed the forces of George A. Custer, who had been instrumental in bringing settlers into the Sioux territory. After Custer and his men were killed in what became known as "Custer's Last Stand," the American people were outraged. The media portrayed

Custer's struggle as a glorious stand against the savage Natives. The *Helena Daily Herald* reported:

> The Indians poured in a murderous fire from all directions, besides the greater portion fought on horseback. Custer, his two brothers, nephew and brother-in-law were killed, and not one of his detachment escaped. Two hundred and seven men were buried in one place, and the number of killed is estimated at three hundred, with only thirty-one wounded.

Public support for Native American removal prompted the United States to aggressively seek out the destruction of Native settlements throughout the Great Plains. The Sioux won a resounding victory over Custer and units of the Seventh Cavalry at Little Bighorn in 1876, but after the Sioux suffered defeat in other conflicts, their chief Sitting Bull surrendered in 1881. They were forced onto reservations, where, facing dire conditions and sure extinction, the Natives began to resort to a practice known as the **Ghost Dance**. The Sioux and other tribes believed it would bring prosperity back to their people and protect them from white people.

> All Indians must dance, everywhere, keep on dancing. Pretty soon in next spring Great Spirit come. He bring back all game of every kind. The game be thick everywhere. All dead Indians come back and live again ... When Great Spirit comes this way, then all the Indians go to mountains, high up away from whites. Whites can't hurt Indians then.

These directions came from Wovoka, a Paiute holy man seen to be bringing a message of salvation to the Sioux. The Sioux prayed for salvation, but only more death and

This photo shows the bodies of murdered Sioux villagers tossed in a mass grave after the Wounded Knee Massacre in South Dakota.

destruction followed. Whites feared the dance and believed it would lead to a revolt, and they demanded that its practice be ended. Sitting Bull supported the Ghost Dance, and on December 15, 1890, he was killed when police forced their way into his house and tried to arrest him. Two weeks later, at Wounded Knee Creek in South Dakota, the United States military was dispatched to round up and disarm a group of fleeing Ghost Dancers. The soldiers created confusion, which led to a gun going off. The army opened fire on the crowds of freezing and starving Natives, made up of men, women, and children. In an instant, 150 people were killed, with the death toll rising to as many as 300 as the soldiers attempted to regain control in the chaos. However, this episode marked a turning point for Native affairs in the West. As most tribes by 1890 had been either imprisoned or wiped out by American forces, the Sioux were the last major resistor of the United States. After the Wounded Knee Massacre, the spirit of the Sioux was broken. In the words of Sioux elder Black Elk, recorded many years later:

> I can still see the butchered women and children lying heaped and scattered all along the crooked gulch as plain as when I saw them with eyes still young. And I can see that something else died there in the bloody mud, and was buried in the blizzard. A people's dream died there. It was a beautiful dream … There is no center any longer, and the sacred tree is dead.

In 1776, Thomas Jefferson wrote in the Declaration of Independence:

> We hold these truths to be self-evident, that all men are created equal, that they are endowed by their Creator with certain unalienable rights, that among these are life, liberty and the pursuit of happiness … When a long train of abuses and usurpations, pursuing invariably the same object, evinces a design to reduce them under absolute despotism, it is their right, it is their duty, to throw off such government, and to provide new guards for their future security.

Certainly, the Native peoples of the American continent were only acting as Jefferson instructed—throwing off despotism, securing their own liberty, and fighting for equality.

Sadly, the United States refused to see the Native Americans' plight this way.

Attempt at Statehood

In 1905, the "Five Civilized Tribes"—Cherokee, Chickasaw, Creek, Seminole, and Choctaw Natives who had cooperated with the American government—met to discuss their independence. They feared forced assimilation, and they wanted to remain free. The tribes proposed that Congress allow the Oklahoma Territory, which housed many Native groups, to become a state for Native Americans. The Sequoyah Constitution mirrored many state constitutions, aiming to consider the Native groups citizens of a state, equally protected by the United States Constitution as a member of the Union. The Sequoyah Constitution began with a preamble, which stated:

> Invoking the blessing of Almighty God and reposing faith in the Constitution and Treaty obligations of the United States, we, the people of the State of Sequoyah, do ordain and establish this Constitution.

However, Congress refused to accept this idea, even though their constitution was American in every way. Instead, representatives defeated the constitution's introduction to Congress. In 1907, Congress declared the Sequoyah Constitution null and void, and they entered Oklahoma into the union as the forty-sixth state. This allowed Congress to add Native territory as full-fledged states, refusing to recognize protest or alternative proposals from Native organizations. New Mexico and Arizona would be added to the Union by 1912, and westward expansion would be complete. As a result, the United States extinguished all resistance from Native Americans. Over the course of two hundred years, it had laid waste to an entire society of free peoples.

Chronology

Dates in green pertain to events discussed in this volume.

September 28, 1542: Juan Rodríguez Cabrillo "discovers" present-day California (although indigenous people had lived there for thousands of years). He claims the region for Spain.

April 30, 1803: The United States under President Thomas Jefferson buys 828,000 square miles (2.1 million square kilometers) of land west of the Mississippi River from France in a deal known as the Louisiana Purchase.

May 14, 1804: Meriwether Lewis and William Clark leave Camp DuBois with the Corps of Discovery to explore the Louisiana Purchase and try to find a water route to the Pacific coast.

December 2, 1823: President James Monroe declares that the American continents "are henceforth not to be considered as subjects for future colonization by any European powers." This principle would become known as the Monroe Doctrine.

May 28, 1830: President Andrew Jackson signs the Indian Removal Act, allowing for the removal of Native Americans from their homelands to unsettled land west of the Mississippi.

1835: Some Cherokees accept land west of the Mississippi and money as payment for agreeing to vacate their land. This leads to the Trail of Tears in 1838, during which thousands of Native Americans perish during a forced march west.

July–August 1845: The term "manifest destiny" is coined by John L. O'Sullivan in an article on the annexation of Texas published in the *United States Magazine and Democratic Review.*

January 24, 1848: James Marshall discovers gold at John Sutter's mill in California. Marshall and Sutter attempt to keep the find secret.

February 2, 1848: Representatives from the United States and Mexico sign the Treaty of Guadalupe Hidalgo, ending the Mexican-American War and ceding more than 500,000 square miles (1.25 million sq km).

December 30, 1853: The United States buys 29,670 square miles (76,845 sq km) from Mexico in what is known as the Gadsden Purchase. The area later becomes part of Arizona and New Mexico.

September 9, 1850: California becomes the thirty-first state.

May 20, 1862: President Abraham Lincoln signs the Homestead Act, which provides settlers 160 acres (65 hectares) of public land west of the Mississippi provided they live on the land for five consecutive years.

July 1, 1862: Congress passes the Pacific Railway Act, which aids in the construction of the transcontinental railroad. The railroad is built between 1863 and 1869. Passengers can now travel from New York to California in just eight days.

September 23, 1862: US troops defeat the Dakotas at the Battle of Wood Lake. The Dakota had attacked people who had trespassed on land granted to them by the US government.

January 1864: The Navajos surrender to Kit Carson at Canyon de Chelly in Arizona. The 8,500 men, women, and children are forced to take the Long Walk to live on a barren reservation called Bosque Redondo.

November 29, 1864: Colorado volunteers slaughter approximately two hundred Cheyennes and Arapahoes in an event known as the Sand Creek Massacre, setting off a full-scale war.

June 25, 1876: Assembled tribes wipe out units of the Seventh Cavalry led by General George Custer at the Battle of Little Bighorn.

October 5, 1877: Chief Joseph of the Nez Percés surrenders after US troops stop his attempt to lead his people to freedom in Canada.

February 8, 1887: President Grover Cleveland signs the Dawes Act, allowing for Native American reservations to be divided into parcels that were given to individuals.

December 29, 1890: American soldiers kill between 150 and 300 Sioux on the Pine Ridge Reservation in the Massacre at Wounded Knee.

Glossary

assimilation The process of forcing Native Americans to adopt white customs, culture, and social norms to incorporate them into the United States population.

Cherokees A nation of Native Americans who lived in the Southeast region but were forcibly relocated by the United States government to areas west of the Mississippi River.

Cheyennes A nation of Native Americans that lived in the Great Plains.

Civil War A conflict between the Northern and Southern states within the United States over slavery and its political effects. The war lasted from 1861 to 1865.

diplomacy The process of negotiating with political leaders of another nation to agree on important issues.

Five Civilized Tribes The Cherokees, Chocktaws, Chickasaws, Creeks (Muskogees), and Seminoles, so-called because they appeared to be assimilating.

genocide The organized extermination of a specific group of people by a government or its leaders.

Ghost Dance A religious ceremony, started by the Paiutes, that aimed to bring back the prosperity of their people.

Indian removal The decades-long process of the United States government of forcing Native Americans from their homelands into other territories and reservations.

manifest destiny The nineteenth-century American belief

that the United States had a God-given destiny to acquire territory spanning from the Atlantic to the Pacific Oceans.

Navajos A nation of Native Americans who lived in pueblos in the Southwest.

Nez Percés A nomadic nation of Native Americans who lived in what is now western Montana, Idaho, Washington, and Oregon. They now live in Idaho.

policy A set of objectives or goals for a political leader, or for government systems dealing with important issues.

reservation Land designated by the United States government for Native Americans, on which they were required to live and often forced to settle by the military.

revolt An organized resistance to government action or authority.

Shawnees A nation of Native Americans who lived in the Northeast and Midwest. They resisted American expansion, aligning themselves with Great Britain during the War of 1812.

Sioux A seminomadic nation of Native Americans that lived in the Great Plains region and resisted American expansion.

slavery In the United States, a system of forced labor applied to minorities, primarily to African Americans but also to Native Americans.

territory An established area of land belonging to a nation or a group of people.

treaty An agreement reached between two nations to end a conflict on terms recognized by both sides.

Further Information

Books

Cozzens, Peter. *The Earth Is Weeping: The Epic Story of the Indian Wars for the American West.* New York: Alfred A. Knopf, 2016.

Dunbar-Ortiz, Roxanne. *An Indigenous Peoples' History of the United States.* Boston: Beacon Press, 2015.

Zinn, Howard. *A People's History of the United States.* New York: HarperCollins Publishers, 2003.

Websites

Library of Congress
"Indians of North America: Selected Resources"
https://www.loc.gov/rr/main/indians_rec_links/overview.html
This guide can help you research Native American history through photos, recordings, maps, and other digital resources.

National Museum of the American Indian
"Education Resources"
http://www.nmai.si.edu/explore/education/resources
This site provides links to different aspects of Native American culture as well as to stories on the history of the indigenous people. Also included are lesson plans for teachers.

Smithsonian Education
"American Indian Heritage Teaching Resources"
http://www.smithsonianeducation.org/educators/resource_library/american_indian_resources.html
The expertise of the Smithsonian Institution allows you to explore reliable resources about a wealth of topics concerning Native Americans.

Bibliography

Books

Brown, Dee. *Bury My Heart at Wounded Knee: An Indian History of the American West.* New York: Open Road Media, 2012.

Hill, Gord. *500 Years of Indigenous Resistance.* Oakland, CA: PM Press, 2009.

Reséndez, Andrés. *The Other Slavery: The Uncovered Story of Indian Enslavement in America.* Boston: Houghton Mifflin Harcourt, 2016.

Ross, John. *The Papers of Chief John Ross, vol 1, 1807–1839.* Gary E. Moulton, ed. Norman, OK: University of Oklahoma Press, 1985.

Online Articles

"Building the First Transcontinental Railroad: Native Americans." Digital Public Library of America. Accessed October 17, 2016. https://dp.la/exhibitions/exhibits/show/transcontinental-railroad/human-impact/native-americans.

Burnett, John G. "A Soldier Recalls the Trail of Tears." Learn NC. Accessed October 17, 2016. http://www.learnnc.org/lp/editions/nchist-newnation/4532.

Burnett, Peter. "State of the State Address." January 6, 1851. The Governor of California: The Governor's Gallery. Accessed October 17, 2016. http://governors.library.ca.gov/addresses/s_01-Burnett2.html.

"Constitution of the Cherokee Nation." 1827. Digital History. Accessed October 17, 2016. http://www.digitalhistory.uh.edu/active_learning/explorations/indian_removal/cherokee_constitution.cfm.

Eastman, Charles A. "Native American Legends: Little Crow—Leader in the Dakota War of 1862." Legends of America. Accessed October 17, 2016. http://www.legendsofamerica.com/na-littlecrow.html.

Fixico, Donald. "Interview: Native Americans." PBS, American Experience: Transconcontintal Railroad. Accessed October 17, 2016. http://www.pbs.org/wgbh/americanexperience/features/interview/tcrr-interview.

"Fort Laramie Treaty, 1868." PBS, New Perspectives on the West. Accessed October 17, 2016. http://www.pbs.org/weta/thewest/resources/archives/four/ftlaram.htm.

"Great Battle with the Indians." *Helena Herald*, July 4, 1876. http://www.astonisher.com/archives/museum/first_newspaper_big_horn.html

Jefferson, Thomas. "Special Message to Congress on Indian Policy." January 18, 1803. Miller Center. Accessed October 25, 2016. http://millercenter.org/president/jefferson/speeches/speech-3476.

"President Jefferson and the Indian Nations." Thomas Jefferson's Monticello. Accessed October 17, 2016. https://www.monticello.org/site/jefferson/president-jefferson-and-indian-nations.

"Sand Creek Massacre: Witness Accounts." The Sand Creek Massacre. Accessed October 17, 2016. http://sandcreekmassacre.net/witness-accounts.

"Treaties Between the United States and Native Americans." Yale Law School: Lillian Goldman Law Library—The Avalon Project. October 17, 2016. http://avalon.law.yale.edu/subject_menus/ntreaty.asp.

Index

Page numbers in **boldface** are illustrations. Entries in **boldface** are glossary terms.

About the Author

ZACHARY DEIBEL is a social studies instructor at Cristo Rey Columbus High School in Columbus, Ohio. He holds a bachelor's degree in history from American University and a master's degree in history from Arkansas State University. He enjoys reading, writing, and thinking about American history, government, and society. He previously wrote a book on Thurgood Marshall for Cavendish Square Publishing.